Now You've Got Me Thinking

A Guided Journal for Girls

SUSANNA BLAKE MURPHY

iUniverse, Inc.
Bloomington

Now You've Got Me Thinking
A Guided Journal for Girls

iUniverse books may be ordered through booksellers or by contacting:

iUniverse
1663 Liberty Drive
Bloomington, IN 47403
www.iuniverse.com
1-800-Authors (1-800-288-4677)

ISBN: 978-1-4502-7311-4 (pbk)
ISBN: 978-1-4502-7312-1 (cloth)
ISBN: 978-1-4502-7313-8 (ebk)

Library of Congress Control Number: 2010918791

Printed in the United States of America

iUniverse rev. date: 3/8/2011

For Margot, my inspiration.

Introduction

Your daughter is growing up. It is a joy to see her becoming a mature and independent young person. However, one sad reality is that, as our children grow, they also begin to encounter confusing situations that challenge their sense of self-worth and test their moral compasses. To make matters even more complicated, it is just at the age when they begin to experience these new, intricate scenarios that they also become more private. As a result, the preteen years can be a confusing and lonely time, especially for girls.

This journal can be a very helpful tool for girls approaching these tumultuous years. Experts throughout the world have recognized the value of keeping a journal. Journaling can help individuals sort through thorny issues. The actual process of putting pen to paper can be a cathartic experience that allows one to release the emotions building inside of her. Additionally, by going back and reading what one has written, one can look at the situation a little more objectively and gain some perspective.

Children can enjoy these tremendous benefits that come from journaling just as much as adults. The tricky part for children (and, in fact, for many adults new to journaling) is figuring out topics on which to write. Journaling does not come naturally to many. This journal, however, simultaneously makes journaling fun for the younger population and subtly and gradually trains girls in the art of journaling.

Your daughter will explore a range of topics on her journey through this journal. Each day, she will be called upon to complete six standard sentences. These standard, or repeated, sentences encourage your child to reflect upon topics that will bolster her self-esteem, make her consider ways in which she can improve upon herself, and prompt her to appreciate what she has.

Following the standard sentences, each day the journal will offer three new and creative sentences for your daughter to complete. At least one of these sentences covers a silly topic meant primarily to keep her engaged and having fun. The two remaining sentences are more probing and geared toward getting your daughter to reflect more deeply. For example, one day the journal states, "One thing my parents don't know about me is ..." This sentence is followed by another that begins, "If I told them, they would probably ..." These types of topics may well prompt careful reflection by your daughter and eventually result in her realizing that sharing such a secret might be more useful and less difficult than she initially thought.

Special efforts have been made in the creation of this journal to make it appealing to its target audience. It is written in an informal manner that is familiar, comfortable, and fun for girls. The font is whimsical, and the serious topics are interspersed with the frivolous. This is all by design. In order to get children of this age group to really want to get involved in this process, it is important that it be engaging. If the child feels that she is being given an assignment by a parent, she is more likely to resist participating or, at least, resist immersing herself in the process. Perhaps not realizing she is being called upon to reflect and self-evaluate will help her to accomplish just that.

This book is a tremendous gift to any girl. By giving this book to a girl you know, you will be helping her build her self-esteem, appreciate what life is offering her, and sort through situations and emotions that can escalate and whirl out of control when left alone in her mind. You will be introducing this child to a lifetime of productive self-reflection. It is an invaluable gift.

Let's Get This Party Started!

Welcome to the **Now You've Got Me Thinking: A Guided Journal for Girls**. So, you probably know what a journal is—a diary, right? And I'm guessing this may not be your first journal, but it will be your first real journal. Sure, you might have been given a journal before, where you haven't really known what to write. Because keeping a journal can be so much fun, you might have gotten excited when you first got it and filled in a page or two. But you probably couldn't always think of what to write, so you stopped writing in it, and it finally ended up under your bed, where it collected a lot of the cat's fur. (Why is cat's fur so awesome when it is actually on your cat rubbing against your cheek when you are going to bed, but so totally gross when it is all balled up and stuck to your old journal when it hangs out under your bed for too long?)

Anyhow, the **Now You've Got Me Thinking: A Guided Journal for Girls** is totally different from any journal you have seen or used before. This one helps you figure out cool stuff to write. It will start with some fun sentences that you'll have an awesome time finishing. (You might even want to use some of these questions for a party game with your closest girlfriends!) This is a place where you can share some great stories, express your worries, and even work out some problems for yourself. You can tell your most private secrets, because this book is just for you.

Here is how it works. Each day gets three pages. Like one of those boring old little kids' journals, or grownups' journals, you start each day with today's date. You've got to have that because it'll be fun to look back at it later and know when it was that you were talking about. And it starts with a little section, "Today I ..." That's where you write a little bit about what happened to you today. You know, "Went to school, got there on time for once. It was raining, so had to have indoor recess ... BORING ... Had gymnastics after school and then did my homework ..." So, that's pretty basic, right? Not much different from those other diaries?

Well, this ultracool journal helps you write some more stuff and really gets you thinking. (See why it's called the **Now You've Got Me Thinking: A Guided Journal for Girls**?) See, then every day it asks you a few questions that will get you to think about your day a little bit more and help you figure out what to write about. Like: I am proud about ..."At gymnastics, I finally made it to the top of the climbing rope and rang the bell. It was really fun, and I was super excited because I have been trying to get all the way up that darn thing since last year and now I finally did it—yeah me!" See? I bet you wouldn't have thought to write about that in one of those old, blank journals. So, there are a few of those questions that you'll get every day. If you don't want to answer all of them every day, then don't ... but give it a try. I bet most days you'll be able to think of something to write.

Then there is room at the end of those sections to get into more details about something big that happened. That's where it says: Now I also need to tell you about... That might be where you write about a worry you're having or a fight that two friends of yours are having. If you write about it, sometimes it will help you sort it out.

Finally, on the third page of each date there are three extras. These are the fun, party game–type topics that really get you thinking, like, If I were an animal I would be a ... "bird, because I love, love, love to sing and fly around and play, but then I think it's pretty cool just to hang out in my bedroom, too." You'll never have trouble answering these ... especially ones like, Sometimes my brother/sister is so ... "annoying. He follows me and my friend Natalie around whenever she comes over after school, and he's always trying to come into my room. Doesn't he know what 'privacy' means?!"

Okay, I know, I know, your mom and dad tell you not to talk about your brother being annoying, that it's mean. Well, guess what? It is okay to write it in this journal for a couple of reasons. First of all, no one is ever going to read it, except for you. It's okay to have mean thoughts about people once in a while, as long as you don't say them to other people and as long as you are working on sorting out those mean thoughts. Second of all, you might feel less annoyed by little Jake, or whoever your annoying younger sibling is, because you've already screamed about it in your journal. And third of all, it might just get you thinking about the next question, which is, But, he is also kind of ... "cute, because he loves to pretend he is a puppy and wags his tail and plays fetch ... like when Mom tells me to put on my slippers and I can send him all the way up to my bedroom to get them because we are just playing fetch, right?"

So, you see, this is a safe and useful place to put all of your thoughts, hopes, and dreams. You will learn that writing down what is going on in your awesome brain can help you work out problems, think about things you want to work hard on, and be happy about all the great things about you. (I mean, who can resist spending a little time thinking about how groovy she is?)

So, I say, set aside a little time to write each day, maybe before bed each night. (Okay, so you might have to go up to your room ten minutes early so your parents don't yell at me for keeping you up so late every night. But I'm serious when I say you'll want to go up to bed, if it gives you a chance to start writing in the hippest of hip, coolest of cool, **Now You've Got Me Thinking: A Guided Journal for Girls**.)

I think you will have fun, and maybe you will begin a lifetime of keeping a journal. Can you just imagine if your mom had been keeping a journal since she was your age? Can you imagine what she would have written about? How long it would be? How much smarter she would be by now?

Have fun and **Write On, Sister!**

WHAT I DID TODAY, _____ 20____.

Today I ...

_____
_____
_____
_____
_____
_____
_____
_____
_____
_____
_____

I am proud about ...

_____
_____
_____
_____
_____
_____
_____
_____
_____

One thing I wish I had handled differently was ...

_____
_____
_____
_____
_____
_____
_____
_____
_____

I helped ...

_____

_____

_____

_____

_____

_____

_____

_____

I got frustrated when ...

_____

_____

_____

_____

_____

_____

_____

_____

Now, I also need to tell you about ...

_____

_____

_____

_____

_____

_____

_____

_____

EXTRAS

I can't wait until ...

_____
_____
_____
_____
_____
_____
_____
_____
_____
_____

My favorite book is ...

_____
_____
_____
_____
_____
_____
_____
_____
_____
_____

One person in school I would like to have a conversation with
is ... because ...

_____
_____
_____
_____
_____
_____
_____
_____
_____

WHAT I DID TODAY, _____ 20___ .

Today I ...

_____
_____
_____
_____
_____
_____
_____
_____
_____
_____
_____

I am proud about ...

_____
_____
_____
_____
_____
_____
_____
_____

One thing I wish I had handled differently was ...

_____
_____
_____
_____
_____
_____
_____
_____
_____

I helped ...

_____
_____
_____
_____
_____
_____
_____
_____
_____

I got frustrated when ...

_____
_____
_____
_____
_____
_____
_____
_____
_____

Now, I also need to tell you about ...

_____
_____
_____
_____
_____
_____
_____
_____
_____

EXTRAS

I wish I could ...

_____

_____

_____

_____

_____

_____

_____

_____

_____

I hate it when...

_____

_____

_____

_____

_____

_____

_____

_____

When my friends say mean things about other people, I usually...

_____

_____

_____

_____

_____

_____

_____

_____

_____

11

WHAT I DID TODAY, _____ 20____ .

Today I ...

_____
_____
_____
_____
_____
_____
_____
_____
_____
_____
_____

I am proud about ...

_____
_____
_____
_____
_____
_____
_____
_____
_____
_____

One thing I wish I had handled differently was ...

_____
_____
_____
_____
_____
_____
_____
_____
_____

I helped ...

_____
_____
_____
_____
_____
_____
_____
_____
_____

I got frustrated when ...

_____
_____
_____
_____
_____
_____
_____
_____
_____

Now, I also need to tell you about ...

_____
_____
_____
_____
_____
_____
_____
_____
_____

EXTRAS

If I could meet anyone in the world it would be ...

_____

_____

_____

_____

_____

_____

_____

_____

_____

_____

My perfect day would be ...

_____

_____

_____

_____

_____

_____

_____

_____

_____

I hope that people think of me as ...

_____

_____

_____

_____

_____

_____

_____

_____

_____

_____

WHAT I DID TODAY, _____ 20____.

Today I ...

_____

_____

_____

_____

_____

_____

_____

_____

_____

_____

I am proud about ...

_____

_____

_____

_____

_____

_____

_____

_____

_____

One thing I wish I had handled differently was ...

_____

_____

_____

_____

_____

_____

_____

_____

_____

I helped ...

_____
_____
_____
_____
_____
_____
_____
_____
_____
_____

I got frustrated when ...

_____
_____
_____
_____
_____
_____
_____
_____
_____
_____

Now, I also need to tell you about ...

_____
_____
_____
_____
_____
_____
_____
_____
_____
_____

EXTRAS

I think my brother/sister_____is so ...

_____
_____
_____
_____
_____
_____
_____
_____
_____
_____

But s/he is also very ...

_____
_____
_____
_____
_____
_____
_____
_____
_____
_____

My favorite movie is ...

_____
_____
_____
_____
_____
_____
_____
_____
_____

WHAT I DID TODAY, _____ 20_____.

Today I ...

_____
_____
_____
_____
_____
_____
_____
_____
_____
_____
_____

I am proud about ...

_____
_____
_____
_____
_____
_____
_____
_____
_____
_____

One thing I wish I had handled differently was ...

_____
_____
_____
_____
_____
_____
_____
_____
_____

I helped ...

_____

_____

_____

_____

_____

_____

_____

_____

_____

I got frustrated when ...

_____

_____

_____

_____

_____

_____

_____

_____

Now, I also need to tell you about ...

_____

_____

_____

_____

_____

_____

_____

_____

_____

EXTRAS

Sometimes, it is so hard to ...

_____
_____
_____
_____
_____
_____
_____
_____
_____
_____

The three words I would use to describe me are ...

_____
_____
_____
_____
_____
_____
_____
_____
_____
_____

If I were an animal I would be a ...

_____
_____
_____
_____
_____
_____
_____
_____
_____
_____

WHAT I DID TODAY, _____ 20____ .

Today I ...

_____
_____
_____
_____
_____
_____
_____
_____
_____
_____

I am proud about ...

_____
_____
_____
_____
_____
_____
_____
_____
_____
_____

One thing I wish I had handled differently was ...

_____
_____
_____
_____
_____
_____
_____
_____
_____

I helped ...

_____
_____
_____
_____
_____
_____
_____
_____
_____
_____

I got frustrated when ...

_____
_____
_____
_____
_____
_____
_____
_____
_____
_____

Now, I also need to tell you about ...

_____
_____
_____
_____
_____
_____
_____
_____
_____
_____

EXTRAS

When my mom or dad won't let me do something I want to do, I feel really ...

_____

_____

_____

_____

_____

_____

_____

_____

_____

But, I've learned the best way to handle that is to ...

_____

_____

_____

_____

_____

_____

_____

_____

_____

Sometimes, it makes sense that they say "no" because ...

_____

_____

_____

_____

_____

_____

_____

_____

_____

WHAT I DID TODAY, _____ 20____ .

Today I ...

_____

_____

_____

_____

_____

_____

_____

_____

_____

_____

_____

I am proud about ...

_____

_____

_____

_____

_____

_____

_____

_____

_____

_____

One thing I wish I had handled differently was ...

_____

_____

_____

_____

_____

_____

_____

_____

_____

I helped ...

_____
_____
_____
_____
_____
_____
_____
_____
_____

I got frustrated when ...

_____
_____
_____
_____
_____
_____
_____
_____
_____

Now, I also need to tell you about ...

_____
_____
_____
_____
_____
_____
_____
_____
_____

EXTRAS

If I could have anything in the world it would be ...

_____
_____
_____
_____
_____
_____
_____
_____
_____
_____

My favorite sport is ...

_____
_____
_____
_____
_____
_____
_____
_____
_____
_____

When people talk about me it makes me feel ...

_____
_____
_____
_____
_____
_____
_____
_____
_____
_____

WHAT I DID TODAY, _____ 20____ .

Today I ...

_____
_____
_____
_____
_____
_____
_____
_____
_____
_____

I am proud about ...

_____
_____
_____
_____
_____
_____
_____
_____
_____
_____

One thing I wish I had handled differently was ...

_____
_____
_____
_____
_____
_____
_____
_____
_____
_____

I helped ...

_____

_____

_____

_____

_____

_____

_____

_____

_____

_____

I got frustrated when ...

_____

_____

_____

_____

_____

_____

_____

_____

_____

_____

Now, I also need to tell you about ...

_____

_____

_____

_____

_____

_____

_____

_____

_____

_____

EXTRAS

The best vacation ever would be ...

_____
_____
_____
_____
_____
_____
_____
_____
_____
_____

I love my brother/sister because ...

_____
_____
_____
_____
_____
_____
_____
_____
_____
_____

One day, I want to try ...

_____
_____
_____
_____
_____
_____
_____
_____
_____
_____

WHAT I DID TODAY, _____ 20____ .

Today I ...

_____
_____
_____
_____
_____
_____
_____
_____
_____

I am proud about ...

_____
_____
_____
_____
_____
_____
_____
_____
_____

One thing I wish I had handled differently was ...

_____
_____
_____
_____
_____
_____
_____
_____
_____

I helped ...

_____
_____
_____
_____
_____
_____
_____
_____
_____
_____

I got frustrated when ...

_____
_____
_____
_____
_____
_____
_____
_____
_____
_____

Now, I also need to tell you about ...

_____
_____
_____
_____
_____
_____
_____
_____
_____
_____
_____

EXTRAS

I think it is embarrassing when ...

_____
_____
_____
_____
_____
_____
_____
_____
_____
_____
_____

The biggest problem in my life right now is ...

_____
_____
_____
_____
_____
_____
_____
_____
_____
_____
_____

The best teacher I've ever had was ...

_____
_____
_____
_____
_____
_____
_____
_____
_____
_____
_____

WHAT I DID TODAY, _____ 20 .

Today I ...

_____

_____

_____

_____

_____

_____

_____

_____

_____

_____

_____

I am proud about ...

_____

_____

_____

_____

_____

_____

_____

_____

_____

_____

One thing I wish I had handled differently was ...

_____

_____

_____

_____

_____

_____

_____

_____

_____

I helped ...

_____
_____
_____
_____
_____
_____
_____
_____
_____

I got frustrated when ...

_____
_____
_____
_____
_____
_____
_____
_____
_____
_____

Now, I also need to tell you about ...

_____
_____
_____
_____
_____
_____
_____
_____
_____
_____

EXTRAS

One of the most fun days I ever had with my mom was ...

_____

_____

_____

_____

_____

_____

_____

_____

_____

_____

If I were granted three wishes, I would wish for ...

_____

_____

_____

_____

_____

_____

_____

_____

_____

_____

When I don't try hard at something it makes me feel ...

_____

_____

_____

_____

_____

_____

_____

_____

_____

_____

WHAT I DID TODAY, _____ 20____ .

Today I ...

_____
_____
_____
_____
_____
_____
_____
_____
_____
_____
_____

I am proud about ...

_____
_____
_____
_____
_____
_____
_____
_____
_____
_____

One thing I wish I had handled differently was ...

_____
_____
_____
_____
_____
_____
_____
_____
_____

I helped ...

_____
_____
_____
_____
_____
_____
_____
_____
_____

I got frustrated when ...

_____
_____
_____
_____
_____
_____
_____
_____
_____

Now, I also need to tell you about ...

_____
_____
_____
_____
_____
_____
_____
_____
_____
_____

EXTRAS

The biggest fight I ever had with a friend was when ...

_____
_____
_____
_____
_____
_____
_____
_____
_____
_____
_____

Maybe it wouldn't have happened if ...

_____
_____
_____
_____
_____
_____
_____
_____
_____
_____

My favorite smell is ...

_____
_____
_____
_____
_____
_____
_____
_____
_____
_____

WHAT I DID TODAY, _____ 20____ .

Today I ...

_____
_____
_____
_____
_____
_____
_____
_____
_____
_____
_____

I am proud about ...

_____
_____
_____
_____
_____
_____
_____
_____
_____
_____

One thing I wish I had handled differently was ...

_____
_____
_____
_____
_____
_____
_____
_____
_____
_____
_____

I helped ...

_____
_____
_____
_____
_____
_____
_____
_____
_____
_____

I got frustrated when ...

_____
_____
_____
_____
_____
_____
_____
_____
_____
_____

Now, I also need to tell you about ...

_____
_____
_____
_____
_____
_____
_____
_____
_____
_____
_____

EXTRAS

One secret that I have never told anyone is ...

_____
_____
_____
_____
_____
_____
_____
_____
_____
_____

I hope when I'm a mom I will be ...

_____
_____
_____
_____
_____
_____
_____
_____

If I could visit anywhere in the world I would go to ... because ...

_____
_____
_____
_____
_____
_____
_____
_____
_____

WHAT I DID TODAY, _____ 20____ .

Today I ...

_____

_____

_____

_____

_____

_____

_____

_____

_____

_____

I am proud about ...

_____

_____

_____

_____

_____

_____

_____

_____

_____

_____

One thing I wish I had handled differently was ...

_____

_____

_____

_____

_____

_____

_____

_____

_____

I helped ...

_____
_____
_____
_____
_____
_____
_____
_____
_____

I got frustrated when ...

_____
_____
_____
_____
_____
_____
_____
_____
_____

Now, I also need to tell you about ...

_____
_____
_____
_____
_____
_____
_____
_____
_____
_____

EXTRAS

The scariest thing I ever did was ...

_____
_____
_____
_____
_____
_____
_____
_____
_____
_____
_____

I think it is sad when ...

_____
_____
_____
_____
_____
_____
_____
_____
_____
_____

When I get older I want to ...

_____
_____
_____
_____
_____
_____
_____
_____
_____
_____
_____

WHAT I DID TODAY, _____ 20____.

Today I ...

_____
_____
_____
_____
_____
_____
_____
_____
_____
_____

I am proud about ...

_____
_____
_____
_____
_____
_____
_____
_____
_____

One thing I wish I had handled differently was ...

_____
_____
_____
_____
_____
_____
_____
_____
_____

I helped ...

_____
_____
_____
_____
_____
_____
_____
_____
_____

I got frustrated when ...

_____
_____
_____
_____
_____
_____
_____
_____
_____

Now, I also need to tell you about ...

_____
_____
_____
_____
_____
_____
_____
_____
_____

EXTRAS

If I ever saw someone I didn't like being bullied at school, I probably would ...

_____

_____

_____

_____

_____

_____

_____

_____

_____

One of the most fun things I ever did with my dad was ...

_____

_____

_____

_____

_____

_____

_____

_____

My favorite part of school is ...

_____

_____

_____

_____

_____

_____

_____

_____

WHAT I DID TODAY, _____ 20____.

Today I ...

_____
_____
_____
_____
_____
_____
_____
_____
_____
_____
_____

I am proud about ...

_____
_____
_____
_____
_____
_____
_____
_____
_____
_____

One thing I wish I had handled differently was ...

_____
_____
_____
_____
_____
_____
_____
_____
_____

I helped ...

_____
_____
_____
_____
_____
_____
_____
_____
_____

I got frustrated when ...

_____
_____
_____
_____
_____
_____
_____
_____
_____

Now, I also need to tell you about ...

_____
_____
_____
_____
_____
_____
_____
_____
_____
_____

EXTRAS

I wish I were better at ...

_____
_____
_____
_____
_____
_____
_____
_____
_____
_____

I love spending time with my grandparents/uncles/aunts ...
because ...

_____
_____
_____
_____
_____
_____
_____
_____
_____
_____

I wish my parents would let me ...

_____
_____
_____
_____
_____
_____
_____
_____
_____

WHAT I DID TODAY, _____ 20____.

Today I ...

_____
_____
_____
_____
_____
_____
_____
_____
_____
_____
_____

I am proud about ...

_____
_____
_____
_____
_____
_____
_____
_____
_____
_____

One thing I wish I had handled differently was ...

_____
_____
_____
_____
_____
_____
_____
_____
_____
_____

I helped ...

_____

_____

_____

_____

_____

_____

_____

_____

_____

I got frustrated when ...

_____

_____

_____

_____

_____

_____

_____

_____

_____

Now, I also need to tell you about ...

_____

_____

_____

_____

_____

_____

_____

_____

_____

EXTRAS

My friend _____ thinks she is _____
but really she is _____. I wonder if I am
wrong about myself in some ways, too. Maybe I am ...

_____

_____

_____

_____

_____

_____

_____

_____

_____

_____

_____

The worst thing that ever happened to me was ...

_____

_____

_____

_____

_____

_____

_____

_____

_____

_____

My favorite singer/band is ...

_____

_____

_____

_____

_____

_____

_____

WHAT I DID TODAY, _____ 20____ .

Today I ...

_____
_____
_____
_____
_____
_____
_____
_____
_____
_____
_____

I am proud about ...

_____
_____
_____
_____
_____
_____
_____
_____
_____
_____

One thing I wish I had handled differently was ...

_____
_____
_____
_____
_____
_____
_____
_____
_____

I helped ...

_____

_____

_____

_____

_____

_____

_____

_____

I got frustrated when ...

_____

_____

_____

_____

_____

_____

_____

_____

Now, I also need to tell you about ...

_____

_____

_____

_____

_____

_____

_____

_____

_____

_____

EXTRAS

I love where I live because ...

_____

_____

_____

_____

_____

_____

_____

_____

_____

When I work hard at something it makes me feel ...

_____

_____

_____

_____

_____

_____

_____

_____

_____

I wish people at school would be more ...

_____

_____

_____

_____

_____

_____

_____

_____

_____

WHAT I DID TODAY, _____ 20 ___.

Today I ...

_____
_____
_____
_____
_____
_____
_____
_____
_____
_____
_____

I am proud about ...

_____
_____
_____
_____
_____
_____
_____
_____
_____
_____

One thing I wish I had handled differently was ...

_____
_____
_____
_____
_____
_____
_____
_____
_____
_____

I helped ...

_____
_____
_____
_____
_____
_____
_____
_____
_____

I got frustrated when ...

_____
_____
_____
_____
_____
_____
_____
_____
_____
_____

Now, I also need to tell you about ...

_____
_____
_____
_____
_____
_____
_____
_____
_____
_____

EXTRAS

Sometimes, I wonder if ...

_____

_____

_____

_____

_____

_____

_____

_____

_____

_____

I wish I had a pet _____, because ...

_____

_____

_____

_____

_____

_____

_____

_____

_____

For my next birthday I want to ...

_____

_____

_____

_____

_____

_____

_____

_____

_____

_____

WHAT I DID TODAY, _____ 20___.

Today I ...

_____

_____

_____

_____

_____

_____

_____

_____

_____

_____

I am proud about ...

_____

_____

_____

_____

_____

_____

_____

_____

_____

_____

One thing I wish I had handled differently was ...

_____

_____

_____

_____

_____

_____

_____

_____

_____

I helped ...

_____
_____
_____
_____
_____
_____
_____
_____
_____

I got frustrated when ...

_____
_____
_____
_____
_____
_____
_____
_____
_____

Now, I also need to tell you about ...

_____
_____
_____
_____
_____
_____
_____
_____
_____
_____

EXTRAS

It is so unfair that ...

_____
_____
_____
_____
_____
_____
_____
_____
_____
_____

But I guess I am lucky because ...

_____
_____
_____
_____
_____
_____
_____
_____
_____

My favorite food is ...

_____
_____
_____
_____
_____
_____

WHAT I DID TODAY, _____ 20____ .

Today I ...

_____
_____
_____
_____
_____
_____
_____
_____
_____
_____

I am proud about ...

_____
_____
_____
_____
_____
_____
_____
_____
_____
_____

One thing I wish I had handled differently was ...

_____
_____
_____
_____
_____
_____
_____
_____
_____

I helped ...

_____
_____
_____
_____
_____
_____
_____
_____
_____
_____

I got frustrated when ...

_____
_____
_____
_____
_____
_____
_____
_____
_____
_____

Now, I also need to tell you about ...

_____
_____
_____
_____
_____
_____
_____
_____
_____
_____

EXTRAS

Something I wish I could tell my parents about but don't think I can is ...

_____
_____
_____
_____
_____
_____
_____
_____
_____
_____

If I told them they would ...

_____
_____
_____
_____
_____
_____
_____
_____

Maybe I could tell them if ...

_____
_____
_____
_____
_____
_____
_____
_____
_____
_____

WHAT I DID TODAY, _____ 20____.

Today I ...

_____
_____
_____
_____
_____
_____
_____
_____
_____
_____
_____

I am proud about ...

_____
_____
_____
_____
_____
_____
_____
_____
_____
_____

One thing I wish I had handled differently was ...

_____
_____
_____
_____
_____
_____
_____
_____
_____

I helped ...

_____
_____
_____
_____
_____
_____
_____
_____
_____

I got frustrated when ...

_____
_____
_____
_____
_____
_____
_____
_____
_____

Now, I also need to tell you about ...

_____
_____
_____
_____
_____
_____
_____
_____
_____
_____

EXTRAS

The funniest thing that ever happened to me was ...

_____
_____
_____
_____
_____
_____
_____
_____
_____
_____
_____

I can't believe I got **so** mad that one time about ...

_____
_____
_____
_____
_____
_____
_____
_____
_____
_____

I think maybe I got so crazy because I ...

_____
_____
_____
_____
_____
_____
_____
_____
_____
_____

WHAT I DID TODAY, _____ 20____.

Today I ...

_____
_____
_____
_____
_____
_____
_____
_____
_____
_____
_____

I am proud about ...

_____
_____
_____
_____
_____
_____
_____
_____
_____
_____
_____

One thing I wish I had handled differently was ...

_____
_____
_____
_____
_____
_____
_____
_____
_____
_____

I helped ...

_____
_____
_____
_____
_____
_____
_____
_____
_____
_____

I got frustrated when ...

_____
_____
_____
_____
_____
_____
_____
_____
_____
_____

Now, I also need to tell you about ...

_____
_____
_____
_____
_____
_____
_____
_____
_____
_____

EXTRAS

When I am really happy I usually...

_____
_____
_____
_____
_____
_____
_____
_____
_____
_____

I really hate it when people ...

_____
_____
_____
_____
_____
_____
_____
_____
_____
_____

The best thing about me is I...

_____
_____
_____
_____
_____
_____
_____
_____
_____
_____

WHAT I DID TODAY, _____ 20____ .

Today I ...

_____
_____
_____
_____
_____
_____
_____
_____
_____
_____

I am proud about ...

_____
_____
_____
_____
_____
_____
_____
_____
_____

One thing I wish I had handled differently was ...

_____
_____
_____
_____
_____
_____
_____
_____
_____

I helped ...

_____
_____
_____
_____
_____
_____
_____
_____
_____
_____

I got frustrated when ...

_____
_____
_____
_____
_____
_____
_____
_____
_____
_____

Now, I also need to tell you about ...

_____
_____
_____
_____
_____
_____
_____
_____
_____
_____

EXTRAS

I hope I never become ...

_____
_____
_____
_____
_____
_____
_____
_____
_____
_____

My favorite breakfast is ...

_____
_____
_____
_____
_____
_____
_____
_____
_____
_____

One of the best things I ever did for someone was ...

_____
_____
_____
_____
_____
_____
_____
_____
_____
_____

WHAT I DID TODAY, _____ 20___ .

Today I ...

_____
_____
_____
_____
_____
_____
_____
_____
_____
_____
_____

I am proud about ...

_____
_____
_____
_____
_____
_____
_____
_____
_____

One thing I wish I had handled differently was ...

_____
_____
_____
_____
_____
_____
_____
_____
_____
_____

I helped ...

_____
_____
_____
_____
_____
_____
_____
_____
_____
_____

I got frustrated when ...

_____
_____
_____
_____
_____
_____
_____
_____
_____
_____
_____

Now, I also need to tell you about ...

_____
_____
_____
_____
_____
_____
_____
_____
_____
_____
_____

EXTRAS

My favorite shoes are ...

_____
_____
_____
_____
_____
_____
_____
_____

I can't believe I used to ...

_____
_____
_____
_____
_____
_____
_____
_____
_____
_____
_____

I am so lucky because ...

_____
_____
_____
_____
_____
_____
_____
_____
_____
_____
_____
_____
_____

WHAT I DID TODAY, _____ 20____ .

Today I ...

_____
_____
_____
_____
_____
_____
_____
_____
_____
_____

I am proud about ...

_____
_____
_____
_____
_____
_____
_____
_____
_____
_____
_____

One thing I wish I had handled differently was ...

_____
_____
_____
_____
_____
_____
_____
_____
_____
_____

I helped ...

_____
_____
_____
_____
_____
_____
_____
_____
_____

I got frustrated when ...

_____
_____
_____
_____
_____
_____
_____
_____
_____

Now, I also need to tell you about ...

_____
_____
_____
_____
_____
_____
_____
_____
_____
_____

EXTRAS

The grossest food I ever tried was ...

_____
_____
_____
_____
_____
_____
_____
_____

The worst day of my life was ...

_____
_____
_____
_____
_____
_____
_____
_____
_____
_____
_____

The best day of my life was ...

_____
_____
_____
_____
_____
_____
_____
_____
_____
_____
_____
_____

WHAT I DID TODAY, _____ 20____.

Today I ...

_____
_____
_____
_____
_____
_____
_____
_____
_____
_____

I am proud about ...

_____
_____
_____
_____
_____
_____
_____
_____
_____
_____

One thing I wish I had handled differently was ...

_____
_____
_____
_____
_____
_____
_____
_____
_____
_____

I helped ...

_____
_____
_____
_____
_____
_____
_____
_____
_____

I got frustrated when ...

_____
_____
_____
_____
_____
_____
_____
_____
_____

Now, I also need to tell you about ...

_____
_____
_____
_____
_____
_____
_____
_____
_____

EXTRAS

On a rainy day I really like to ...

_____
_____
_____
_____
_____
_____
_____
_____
_____

I wish my mom weren't so ...

_____
_____
_____
_____
_____
_____
_____
_____
_____

But, I do like that she is ...

_____
_____
_____
_____
_____
_____
_____
_____
_____

WHAT I DID TODAY, _____ 20___.

Today I ...

_____
_____
_____
_____
_____
_____
_____
_____
_____
_____
_____

I am proud about ...

_____
_____
_____
_____
_____
_____
_____
_____
_____
_____

One thing I wish I had handled differently was ...

_____
_____
_____
_____
_____
_____
_____
_____
_____
_____

I helped ...

_____
_____
_____
_____
_____
_____
_____
_____
_____

I got frustrated when ...

_____
_____
_____
_____
_____
_____
_____
_____
_____

Now, I also need to tell you about ...

_____
_____
_____
_____
_____
_____
_____
_____
_____

EXTRAS

The biggest mistake I ever made was ...

_____

_____

_____

_____

_____

_____

_____

_____

_____

_____

_____

_____

As I get older, I think I am becoming more ...

_____

_____

_____

_____

_____

_____

_____

_____

_____

_____

_____

My favorite thing to wear to bed is ...

_____

_____

_____

_____

WHAT I DID TODAY, _____ 20____.

Today I ...

_____
_____
_____
_____
_____
_____
_____
_____
_____
_____

I am proud about ...

_____
_____
_____
_____
_____
_____
_____
_____
_____
_____

One thing I wish I had handled differently was ...

_____
_____
_____
_____
_____
_____
_____
_____
_____

I helped ...

_____
_____
_____
_____
_____
_____
_____
_____
_____

I got frustrated when ...

_____
_____
_____
_____
_____
_____
_____
_____
_____

Now, I also need to tell you about ...

_____
_____
_____
_____
_____
_____
_____
_____
_____
_____

EXTRAS

I am not very good at ...

_____
_____
_____
_____
_____
_____
_____
_____
_____

I am pretty good at ...

_____
_____
_____
_____
_____
_____
_____
_____
_____

I am great at ...

_____
_____
_____
_____
_____
_____
_____
_____
_____

WHAT I DID TODAY, _____ 20____ .

Today I ...

_____
_____
_____
_____
_____
_____
_____
_____
_____
_____
_____

I am proud about ...

_____
_____
_____
_____
_____
_____
_____
_____
_____
_____

One thing I wish I had handled differently was ...

_____
_____
_____
_____
_____
_____
_____
_____
_____
_____

I helped ...

_____
_____
_____
_____
_____
_____
_____
_____

I got frustrated when ...

_____
_____
_____
_____
_____
_____
_____
_____
_____

Now, I also need to tell you about ...

_____
_____
_____
_____
_____
_____
_____
_____
_____

EXTRAS

The chore I hate to do the most is ...

_____

_____

_____

_____

_____

_____

_____

_____

_____

The chore I don't really mind doing is ...

_____

_____

_____

_____

_____

_____

_____

_____

_____

I think people should be more ...

_____

_____

_____

_____

_____

_____

_____

_____

WHAT I DID TODAY, _____ 20_____ .

Today I ...

_____

_____

_____

_____

_____

_____

_____

_____

_____

_____

I am proud about ...

_____

_____

_____

_____

_____

_____

_____

_____

One thing I wish I had handled differently was ...

_____

_____

_____

_____

_____

_____

_____

_____

I helped ...

_____
_____
_____
_____
_____
_____
_____
_____
_____
_____

I got frustrated when ...

_____
_____
_____
_____
_____
_____
_____
_____
_____
_____

Now, I also need to tell you about ...

_____
_____
_____
_____
_____
_____
_____
_____
_____

EXTRAS

I wish my dad weren't so ...

_____

_____

_____

_____

_____

_____

_____

_____

_____

But I'm glad my dad is ...

_____

_____

_____

_____

_____

_____

_____

_____

_____

If I could have a superpower it would be ...

_____

_____

_____

_____

_____

_____

_____

_____

_____

WHAT I DID TODAY, _____ 20___ .

Today I ...

_____

_____

_____

_____

_____

_____

_____

_____

_____

_____

I am proud about ...

_____

_____

_____

_____

_____

_____

_____

_____

_____

One thing I wish I had handled differently was ...

_____

_____

_____

_____

_____

_____

_____

_____

_____

I helped ...

_____

_____

_____

_____

_____

_____

_____

_____

I got frustrated when ...

_____

_____

_____

_____

_____

_____

_____

_____

Now, I also need to tell you about ...

_____

_____

_____

_____

_____

_____

_____

_____

_____

EXTRAS

When I'm 16 I think I'll be ...

_____

_____

_____

_____

_____

_____

_____

_____

_____

_____

It is important to me that my friends be ...

_____

_____

_____

_____

_____

_____

_____

_____

_____

_____

I think a fun job would be ...

_____

_____

_____

_____

_____

_____

_____

_____

_____

_____

WHAT I DID TODAY, _____ 20___.

Today I ...

_____
_____
_____
_____
_____
_____
_____
_____
_____
_____

I am proud about ...

_____
_____
_____
_____
_____
_____
_____
_____
_____
_____

One thing I wish I had handled differently was ...

_____
_____
_____
_____
_____
_____
_____
_____
_____

I helped ...

_____

_____

_____

_____

_____

_____

_____

_____

_____

I got frustrated when ...

_____

_____

_____

_____

_____

_____

_____

_____

Now, I also need to tell you about ...

_____

_____

_____

_____

_____

_____

_____

_____

_____

EXTRAS

I love to go to ...

_____

_____

_____

_____

_____

_____

_____

_____

_____

_____

One thing that frustrates me about my best friend is ...

_____

_____

_____

_____

_____

_____

_____

_____

_____

_____

The best thing about my best friend is ...

_____

_____

_____

_____

_____

_____

_____

_____

_____

_____

WHAT I DID TODAY, _____ 20____.

Today I ...

_____
_____
_____
_____
_____
_____
_____
_____
_____
_____

I am proud about ...

_____
_____
_____
_____
_____
_____
_____
_____
_____

One thing I wish I had handled differently was ...

_____
_____
_____
_____
_____
_____
_____
_____
_____

I helped ...

_____
_____
_____
_____
_____
_____
_____
_____
_____

I got frustrated when ...

_____
_____
_____
_____
_____
_____
_____
_____
_____

Now, I also need to tell you about ...

_____
_____
_____
_____
_____
_____
_____
_____
_____

EXTRAS

My favorite kind of candy is ...

_____
_____
_____
_____
_____
_____

I would like to try to be more ...

_____
_____
_____
_____
_____
_____
_____
_____
_____

I make my parents proud when I ...

_____
_____
_____
_____
_____
_____
_____
_____
_____
_____
_____
_____

WHAT I DID TODAY, _____ 20____.

Today I ...

_____

_____

_____

_____

_____

_____

_____

_____

_____

_____

_____

I am proud about ...

_____

_____

_____

_____

_____

_____

_____

_____

_____

One thing I wish I had handled differently was ...

_____

_____

_____

_____

_____

_____

_____

_____

_____

I helped ...

_____
_____
_____
_____
_____
_____
_____
_____
_____
_____

I got frustrated when ...

_____
_____
_____
_____
_____
_____
_____
_____
_____
_____

Now, I also need to tell you about ...

_____
_____
_____
_____
_____
_____
_____
_____
_____
_____
_____

EXTRAS

I could work harder at ...

_____

_____

_____

_____

_____

_____

_____

_____

_____

My friends like me because I am ...

_____

_____

_____

_____

_____

_____

_____

_____

_____

My favorite TV show is ...

_____

_____

_____

_____

_____

_____

_____

_____

_____

WHAT I DID TODAY, _____ 20____ .

Today I ...

_____

_____

_____

_____

_____

_____

_____

_____

_____

_____

I am proud about ...

_____

_____

_____

_____

_____

_____

_____

_____

_____

One thing I wish I had handled differently was ...

_____

_____

_____

_____

_____

_____

_____

_____

_____

I helped ...

_____
_____
_____
_____
_____
_____
_____
_____

I got frustrated when ...

_____
_____
_____
_____
_____
_____
_____
_____

Now, I also need to tell you about ...

_____
_____
_____
_____
_____
_____
_____
_____
_____

EXTRAS

The hardest thing about being a kid is ...

_____
_____
_____
_____
_____
_____
_____
_____
_____

The best part about being a kid is ...

_____
_____
_____
_____
_____
_____
_____
_____
_____

If I could have any pet in the world it would be a ...

_____
_____
_____
_____
_____
_____
_____
_____
_____

WHAT I DID TODAY, _____ 20____.

Today I ...

_____
_____
_____
_____
_____
_____
_____
_____
_____
_____
_____

I am proud about ...

_____
_____
_____
_____
_____
_____
_____
_____
_____
_____

One thing I wish I had handled differently was ...

_____
_____
_____
_____
_____
_____
_____
_____
_____
_____

I helped ...

_____
_____
_____
_____
_____
_____
_____
_____
_____
_____

I got frustrated when ...

_____
_____
_____
_____
_____
_____
_____
_____
_____
_____

Now, I also need to tell you about ...

_____
_____
_____
_____
_____
_____
_____
_____
_____
_____

EXTRAS

It really hurts my feelings when ...

_____
_____
_____
_____
_____
_____
_____
_____
_____
_____
_____

I think I could be good at ...

_____
_____
_____
_____
_____
_____
_____
_____
_____
_____
_____

When I'm scared I usually ...

_____
_____
_____
_____
_____
_____
_____
_____
_____
_____
_____

WHAT I DID TODAY, _____ 20____.

Today I ...

_____
_____
_____
_____
_____
_____
_____
_____
_____
_____
_____

I am proud about ...

_____
_____
_____
_____
_____
_____
_____
_____
_____
_____

One thing I wish I had handled differently was ...

_____
_____
_____
_____
_____
_____
_____
_____
_____

I helped ...

_____
_____
_____
_____
_____
_____
_____
_____
_____

I got frustrated when ...

_____
_____
_____
_____
_____
_____
_____
_____
_____

Now, I also need to tell you about ...

_____
_____
_____
_____
_____
_____
_____
_____
_____

EXTRAS

One thing my friends would be surprised to know about me is ...

_____

_____

_____

_____

_____

_____

_____

_____

One thing my parents would be surprised to know about me is ...

_____

_____

_____

_____

_____

_____

_____

_____

When I try to go to sleep, I usually think about ...

_____

_____

_____

_____

_____

_____

_____

_____

_____

WHAT I DID TODAY, _____ 20____.

Today I ...

_____
_____
_____
_____
_____
_____
_____
_____
_____
_____
_____

I am proud about ...

_____
_____
_____
_____
_____
_____
_____
_____
_____
_____
_____

One thing I wish I had handled differently was ...

_____
_____
_____
_____
_____
_____
_____
_____
_____
_____

I helped ...

_____

_____

_____

_____

_____

_____

_____

_____

_____

I got frustrated when ...

_____

_____

_____

_____

_____

_____

_____

_____

Now, I also need to tell you about ...

_____

_____

_____

_____

_____

_____

_____

_____

_____

EXTRAS

The best thing about school is ...

_____
_____
_____
_____
_____
_____
_____
_____
_____

The hardest thing about school is ...

_____
_____
_____
_____
_____
_____
_____
_____
_____

I think it would be really hard to ...

_____
_____
_____
_____
_____
_____
_____
_____
_____

WHAT I DID TODAY, _____ 20____ .

Today I ...

_____
_____
_____
_____
_____
_____
_____
_____
_____
_____
_____

I am proud about ...

_____
_____
_____
_____
_____
_____
_____
_____
_____
_____

One thing I wish I had handled differently was ...

_____
_____
_____
_____
_____
_____
_____
_____
_____
_____

I helped ...

_____
_____
_____
_____
_____
_____
_____
_____
_____

I got frustrated when ...

_____
_____
_____
_____
_____
_____
_____
_____
_____

Now, I also need to tell you about ...

_____
_____
_____
_____
_____
_____
_____
_____
_____
_____

EXTRAS

If I were stranded on a deserted island with three people, I would like those three people to be ...

_____
_____
_____
_____
_____
_____
_____
_____
_____
_____

I wish I had never ...

_____
_____
_____
_____
_____
_____
_____
_____
_____

One thing I would never do is ...

_____
_____
_____
_____
_____
_____
_____
_____
_____

WHAT I DID TODAY, _____ 20____.

Today I ...

_____
_____
_____
_____
_____
_____
_____
_____
_____
_____
_____

I am proud about ...

_____
_____
_____
_____
_____
_____
_____
_____
_____

One thing I wish I had handled differently was ...

_____
_____
_____
_____
_____
_____
_____
_____
_____

I helped ...

_____
_____
_____
_____
_____
_____
_____
_____
_____

I got frustrated when ...

_____
_____
_____
_____
_____
_____
_____
_____
_____

Now, I also need to tell you about ...

_____
_____
_____
_____
_____
_____
_____
_____
_____

EXTRAS

The best thing about reading is ...

_____
_____
_____
_____
_____
_____
_____
_____
_____
_____

One way I deal with being angry is ...

_____
_____
_____
_____
_____
_____
_____
_____
_____
_____

Another good way to handle being angry might be ...

_____
_____
_____
_____
_____
_____
_____
_____
_____
_____

WHAT I DID TODAY, _____ 20____ .

Today I ...

_____
_____
_____
_____
_____
_____
_____
_____
_____

I am proud about ...

_____
_____
_____
_____
_____
_____
_____
_____
_____

One thing I wish I had handled differently was ...

_____
_____
_____
_____
_____
_____
_____
_____
_____

I helped ...

_____
_____
_____
_____
_____
_____
_____
_____
_____

I got frustrated when ...

_____
_____
_____
_____
_____
_____
_____
_____
_____
_____

Now, I also need to tell you about ...

_____
_____
_____
_____
_____
_____
_____
_____
_____
_____

EXTRAS

My perfect Summer day would be to ...

_____

_____

_____

_____

_____

_____

_____

_____

_____

If I heard that a friend of mine was saying things about me that
were not very nice, I would ...

_____

_____

_____

_____

_____

_____

_____

_____

_____

_____

The hardest thing that I ever did was ...

_____

_____

_____

_____

_____

_____

_____

_____

_____

WHAT I DID TODAY, _____ 20____ .

Today I ...

_____
_____
_____
_____
_____
_____
_____
_____
_____
_____
_____

I am proud about ...

_____
_____
_____
_____
_____
_____
_____
_____
_____

One thing I wish I had handled differently was ...

_____
_____
_____
_____
_____
_____
_____
_____
_____

I helped ...

_____
_____
_____
_____
_____
_____
_____
_____
_____

I got frustrated when ...

_____
_____
_____
_____
_____
_____
_____
_____
_____

Now, I also need to tell you about ...

_____
_____
_____
_____
_____
_____
_____
_____
_____
_____

EXTRAS

The hardest secret I ever had to keep was ...

_____

_____

_____

_____

_____

_____

_____

_____

_____

I wish my parents didn't worry so much about ...

_____

_____

_____

_____

_____

_____

_____

_____

_____

I wish I didn't worry so much about ...

_____

_____

_____

_____

_____

_____

_____

_____

_____

WHAT I DID TODAY, _____ 20____.

Today I ...

_____
_____
_____
_____
_____
_____
_____
_____
_____
_____

I am proud about ...

_____
_____
_____
_____
_____
_____
_____
_____
_____

One thing I wish I had handled differently was ...

_____
_____
_____
_____
_____
_____
_____
_____
_____

I helped ...

_____
_____
_____
_____
_____
_____
_____
_____
_____
_____

I got frustrated when ...

_____
_____
_____
_____
_____
_____
_____
_____
_____
_____

Now, I also need to tell you about ...

_____
_____
_____
_____
_____
_____
_____
_____
_____
_____

EXTRAS

I get so tired of ...

_____
_____
_____
_____
_____
_____
_____
_____
_____
_____
_____

Maybe I wouldn't get so tired of that if ...

_____
_____
_____
_____
_____
_____
_____
_____
_____
_____

My favorite dinner is ...

_____
_____
_____
_____
_____
_____
_____
_____
_____
_____

WHAT I DID TODAY, _____ 20____.

Today I ...

_____

_____

_____

_____

_____

_____

_____

_____

_____

_____

I am proud about ...

_____

_____

_____

_____

_____

_____

_____

_____

_____

_____

One thing I wish I had handled differently was ...

_____

_____

_____

_____

_____

_____

_____

_____

_____

I helped ...

_____

_____

_____

_____

_____

_____

_____

_____

_____

_____

I got frustrated when ...

_____

_____

_____

_____

_____

_____

_____

_____

_____

_____

Now, I also need to tell you about ...

_____

_____

_____

_____

_____

_____

_____

_____

_____

_____

EXTRAS

I think writing in this journal is ...

_____
_____
_____
_____
_____
_____
_____
_____
_____

One person at school whom I admire is ...

_____
_____
_____
_____
_____
_____
_____
_____
_____
_____

When people copy me it makes me feel ...

_____
_____
_____
_____
_____
_____
_____
_____
_____

WHAT I DID TODAY, _____ 20____ .

Today I ...

_____

_____

_____

_____

_____

_____

_____

_____

_____

_____

_____

I am proud about ...

_____

_____

_____

_____

_____

_____

_____

_____

_____

_____

One thing I wish I had handled differently was ...

_____

_____

_____

_____

_____

_____

_____

_____

_____

I helped ...

_____

_____

_____

_____

_____

_____

_____

_____

_____

I got frustrated when ...

_____

_____

_____

_____

_____

_____

_____

_____

_____

Now, I also need to tell you about ...

_____

_____

_____

_____

_____

_____

_____

_____

_____

_____

EXTRAS

When two friends of mine aren't getting along, I ...

_____
_____
_____
_____
_____
_____
_____
_____
_____

My favorite thing to do with a group of friends is ...

_____
_____
_____
_____
_____
_____
_____
_____
_____

My favorite friend's house to go to is ...

_____
_____
_____
_____
_____
_____
_____
_____
_____

WHAT I DID TODAY, _____ 20___ .

Today I ...

_____
_____
_____
_____
_____
_____
_____
_____
_____
_____

I am proud about ...

_____
_____
_____
_____
_____
_____
_____
_____
_____

One thing I wish I had handled differently was ...

_____
_____
_____
_____
_____
_____
_____
_____

I helped ...

_____

_____

_____

_____

_____

_____

_____

_____

I got frustrated when ...

_____

_____

_____

_____

_____

_____

_____

_____

Now, I also need to tell you about ...

_____

_____

_____

_____

_____

_____

_____

_____

_____

EXTRAS

The last time I got REALLY mad was when ...

The last time I laughed REALLY hard was ...

The most fun thing I do with my family is ...

WHAT I DID TODAY, _____ 20____ .

Today I ...

_____

_____

_____

_____

_____

_____

_____

_____

_____

I am proud about ...

_____

_____

_____

_____

_____

_____

_____

_____

_____

_____

_____

One thing I wish I had handled differently was ...

_____

_____

_____

_____

_____

_____

_____

_____

_____

I helped ...

_____
_____
_____
_____
_____
_____
_____
_____
_____

I got frustrated when ...

_____
_____
_____
_____
_____
_____
_____
_____
_____

Now, I also need to tell you about ...

_____
_____
_____
_____
_____
_____
_____
_____
_____

EXTRAS

I don't know why people at school care so much about ...

_____

_____

_____

_____

_____

_____

_____

_____

_____

I wish people cared more about ...

_____

_____

_____

_____

_____

_____

_____

_____

One thing I would like to do to make the world a better place is ...

_____

_____

_____

_____

_____

_____

_____

_____

WHAT I DID TODAY, _____ 20____.

Today I ...

_____
_____
_____
_____
_____
_____
_____
_____
_____
_____

I am proud about ...

_____
_____
_____
_____
_____
_____
_____
_____
_____

One thing I wish I had handled differently was ...

_____
_____
_____
_____
_____
_____
_____
_____
_____

I helped ...

_____
_____
_____
_____
_____
_____
_____
_____
_____

I got frustrated when ...

_____
_____
_____
_____
_____
_____
_____
_____
_____

Now, I also need to tell you about ...

_____
_____
_____
_____
_____
_____
_____
_____
_____
_____

EXTRAS

One thing my parents have done that I would like to do is ...

_____
_____
_____
_____
_____
_____
_____
_____
_____
_____

One thing I think is strange is ...

_____
_____
_____
_____
_____
_____
_____
_____
_____
_____

It is so gross when ...

_____
_____
_____
_____
_____
_____
_____
_____
_____
_____

WHAT I DID TODAY, _____ 20____ .

Today I ...

_____
_____
_____
_____
_____
_____
_____
_____
_____
_____

I am proud about ...

_____
_____
_____
_____
_____
_____
_____
_____
_____
_____

One thing I wish I had handled differently was ...

_____
_____
_____
_____
_____
_____
_____
_____
_____
_____

I helped ...

_____
_____
_____
_____
_____
_____
_____
_____
_____

I got frustrated when ...

_____
_____
_____
_____
_____
_____
_____
_____
_____

Now, I also need to tell you about ...

_____
_____
_____
_____
_____
_____
_____
_____
_____
_____

EXTRAS

Sometimes, when people seem mean, they really are just ...

_____
_____
_____
_____
_____
_____
_____
_____
_____
_____

Acting in a play is really ...

_____
_____
_____
_____
_____
_____
_____
_____
_____
_____

I feel proud of my mom because ...

_____
_____
_____
_____
_____
_____
_____
_____
_____
_____

WHAT I DID TODAY, _____ 20____.

Today I ...

_____

_____

_____ .

_____

_____

_____

_____

_____

_____

_____

I am proud about ...

_____

_____

_____

_____

_____

_____

_____

_____

_____

One thing I wish I had handled differently was ...

_____

_____

_____

_____

_____

_____

_____

_____

I helped ...

_____
_____
_____
_____
_____
_____
_____
_____
_____

I got frustrated when ...

_____
_____
_____
_____
_____
_____
_____
_____
_____

Now, I also need to tell you about ...

_____
_____
_____
_____
_____
_____
_____
_____
_____
_____

EXTRAS

Getting muddy is ...

_____

_____

_____

_____

_____

_____

_____

_____

_____

_____

One teacher I hope I'll have one day is ...

_____

_____

_____

_____

_____

_____

_____

_____

_____

_____

School is ...

_____

_____

_____

_____

_____

_____

_____

_____

_____

_____

My life would be so much worse if ...

_____
_____
_____
_____
_____
_____
_____
_____
_____
_____
_____

WHAT I DID TODAY, _____ 20___.

Today I ...

_____
_____
_____
_____
_____
_____
_____
_____
_____
_____

I am proud about ...

_____
_____
_____
_____
_____
_____
_____
_____
_____

One thing I wish I had handled differently was ...

_____
_____
_____
_____
_____
_____
_____
_____
_____

I helped ...

_____
_____
_____
_____
_____
_____
_____
_____
_____

I got frustrated when ...

_____
_____
_____
_____
_____
_____
_____
_____
_____

Now, I also need to tell you about ...

_____
_____
_____
_____
_____
_____
_____
_____
_____
_____

EXTRAS

I wish my family spent more time ...

_____
_____
_____
_____
_____
_____
_____
_____
_____
_____

My favorite day of the week is ...

_____
_____
_____
_____
_____
_____
_____
_____
_____
_____

If I could go out to dinner and spend the night in a hotel alone or have a campfire and camp out with friends I would choose ...

_____
_____
_____
_____
_____
_____
_____
_____
_____

WHAT I DID TODAY, _____ 20____ .

Today I ...

_____

_____

_____

_____

_____

_____

_____

_____

_____

_____

I am proud about ...

_____

_____

_____

_____

_____

_____

_____

_____

_____

One thing I wish I had handled differently was ...

_____

_____

_____

_____

_____

_____

_____

_____

I helped ...

_____
_____
_____
_____
_____
_____
_____
_____
_____

I got frustrated when ...

_____
_____
_____
_____
_____
_____
_____
_____
_____

Now, I also need to tell you about ...

_____
_____
_____
_____
_____
_____
_____
_____
_____

EXTRAS

The most fun after-school activity I ever did was ...

_____

_____

_____

_____

_____

_____

_____

_____

_____

Sometimes I worry that ...

_____

_____

_____

_____

_____

_____

_____

_____

_____

One thing that might help that worry is ...

_____

_____

_____

_____

_____

_____

_____

_____

_____

WHAT I DID TODAY, _____ 20____ .

Today I ...

_____

_____

_____

_____

_____

_____

_____

_____

_____

_____

_____

I am proud about ...

_____

_____

_____

_____

_____

_____

_____

_____

_____

_____

One thing I wish I had handled differently was ...

_____

_____

_____

_____

_____

_____

_____

_____

_____

I helped ...

_____
_____
_____
_____
_____
_____
_____
_____
_____

I got frustrated when ...

_____
_____
_____
_____
_____
_____
_____
_____
_____

Now, I also need to tell you about ...

_____
_____
_____
_____
_____
_____
_____
_____
_____
_____

EXTRAS

One thing I don't understand about my best friend is ...

_____
_____
_____
_____
_____
_____
_____
_____
_____

One thing my best friend might not understand about me is ...

_____
_____
_____
_____
_____
_____
_____
_____
_____

I am so happy that I get to ....

_____
_____
_____
_____
_____
_____
_____
_____
_____

WHAT I DID TODAY, _____ 20____ .

Today I ...

_____
_____
_____
_____
_____
_____
_____
_____
_____
_____

I am proud about ...

_____
_____
_____
_____
_____
_____
_____
_____
_____
_____

One thing I wish I had handled differently was ...

_____
_____
_____
_____
_____
_____
_____
_____

I helped ...

_____
_____
_____
_____
_____
_____
_____
_____
_____

I got frustrated when ...

_____
_____
_____
_____
_____
_____
_____
_____
_____

Now, I also need to tell you about ...

_____
_____
_____
_____
_____
_____
_____
_____
_____
_____

EXTRAS

I wish I could spend more time with ...

_____
_____
_____
_____
_____
_____
_____
_____
_____

The best part about my dad is that he ...

_____
_____
_____
_____
_____
_____
_____
_____
_____

My favorite room in my house is ...

_____
_____
_____
_____
_____
_____
_____
_____
_____

WHAT I DID TODAY, _____ 20____.

Today I ...

_____
_____
_____
_____
_____
_____
_____
_____
_____
_____
_____

I am proud about ...

_____
_____
_____
_____
_____
_____
_____
_____
_____
_____

One thing I wish I had handled differently was ...

_____
_____
_____
_____
_____
_____
_____
_____
_____
_____

I helped ...

_____
_____
_____
_____
_____
_____
_____
_____
_____

I got frustrated when ...

_____
_____
_____
_____
_____
_____
_____
_____
_____

Now, I also need to tell you about ...

_____
_____
_____
_____
_____
_____
_____
_____
_____
_____

EXTRAS

The night before the first day of school I usually feel ...

_____
_____
_____
_____
_____
_____
_____
_____
_____
_____

I wish my grandparents ...

_____
_____
_____
_____
_____
_____
_____
_____
_____
_____

I think it is hard to ...

_____
_____
_____
_____
_____
_____
_____
_____
_____
_____

WHAT I DID TODAY, _____ 20____.

Today I ...

_____
_____
_____
_____
_____
_____
_____
_____
_____
_____
_____

I am proud about ...

_____
_____
_____
_____
_____
_____
_____
_____
_____
_____
_____

One thing I wish I had handled differently was ...

_____
_____
_____
_____
_____
_____
_____
_____
_____
_____

I helped ...

_____
_____
_____
_____
_____
_____
_____
_____
_____

I got frustrated when ...

_____
_____
_____
_____
_____
_____
_____
_____
_____

Now, I also need to tell you about ...

_____
_____
_____
_____
_____
_____
_____
_____
_____
_____

EXTRAS

One thing I think is scary is ...

_____
_____
_____
_____
_____
_____
_____
_____
_____
_____
_____

I think I should ask my parents to help me more with ...

_____
_____
_____
_____
_____
_____
_____
_____
_____
_____
_____

I think it is funny when ...

_____
_____
_____
_____
_____
_____
_____
_____
_____
_____

WHAT I DID TODAY, _____ 20 ___.

Today I ...

_____
_____
_____
_____
_____
_____
_____
_____
_____
_____

I am proud about ...

_____
_____
_____
_____
_____
_____
_____
_____
_____
_____

One thing I wish I had handled differently was ...

_____
_____
_____
_____
_____
_____
_____
_____
_____

I helped ...

_____
_____
_____
_____
_____
_____
_____
_____
_____

I got frustrated when ...

_____
_____
_____
_____
_____
_____
_____
_____
_____
_____

Now, I also need to tell you about ...

_____
_____
_____
_____
_____
_____
_____
_____
_____
_____

EXTRAS

I will never forget the time I ...

_____

_____

_____

_____

_____

_____

_____

_____

_____

_____

One thing I don't really understand is ...

_____

_____

_____

_____

_____

_____

_____

_____

_____

_____

I wonder what it will be like the first time I ...

_____

_____

_____

_____

_____

_____

_____

_____

_____

_____

WHAT I DID TODAY, _____ 20____.

Today I ...

_____
_____
_____
_____
_____
_____
_____
_____
_____
_____
_____

I am proud about ...

_____
_____
_____
_____
_____
_____
_____
_____
_____
_____

One thing I wish I had handled differently was ...

_____
_____
_____
_____
_____
_____
_____
_____
_____

I helped ...

_____
_____
_____
_____
_____
_____
_____
_____
_____

I got frustrated when ...

_____
_____
_____
_____
_____
_____
_____
_____
_____

Now, I also need to tell you about ...

_____
_____
_____
_____
_____
_____
_____
_____
_____

EXTRAS

The best holiday is ...

_____
_____
_____
_____
_____
_____
_____
_____
_____

When I am really worried about something, I usually ...

_____
_____
_____
_____
_____
_____
_____
_____
_____

The funniest movie I ever saw was ...

_____
_____
_____
_____
_____
_____
_____
_____
_____

WHAT I DID TODAY, _____ 20 ___ .

Today I ...

_____
_____
_____
_____
_____
_____
_____
_____
_____

I am proud about ...

_____
_____
_____
_____
_____
_____
_____
_____
_____

One thing I wish I had handled differently was ...

_____
_____
_____
_____
_____
_____
_____
_____
_____

I helped ...

_____
_____
_____
_____
_____
_____
_____
_____
_____

I got frustrated when ...

_____
_____
_____
_____
_____
_____
_____
_____
_____

Now, I also need to tell you about ...

_____
_____
_____
_____
_____
_____
_____
_____
_____

EXTRAS

The best day of the school year is ...

_____
_____
_____
_____
_____
_____
_____
_____
_____
_____

When I am grown up I hope that I will be ...

_____
_____
_____
_____
_____
_____
_____
_____
_____
_____

When someone lies to me I ...

_____
_____
_____
_____
_____
_____
_____
_____
_____
_____

WHAT I DID TODAY, _____ 20_____.

Today I ...

_____
_____
_____
_____
_____
_____
_____
_____
_____
_____

I am proud about ...

_____
_____
_____
_____
_____
_____
_____
_____
_____

One thing I wish I had handled differently was ...

_____
_____
_____
_____
_____
_____
_____
_____

I helped ...

_____

_____

_____

_____

_____

_____

_____

_____

_____

I got frustrated when ...

_____

_____

_____

_____

_____

_____

_____

_____

_____

Now, I also need to tell you about ...

_____

_____

_____

_____

_____

_____

_____

_____

_____

_____

EXTRAS

If I were a boy I would ...

_____
_____
_____
_____
_____
_____
_____
_____
_____
_____

One thing I miss about being a little kid is ...

_____
_____
_____
_____
_____
_____
_____
_____
_____
_____

When I have a babysitter, I feel ...

_____
_____
_____
_____
_____
_____
_____
_____
_____
_____

WHAT I DID TODAY, _____ 20___.

Today I ...

_____
_____
_____
_____
_____
_____
_____
_____
_____
_____
_____

I am proud about ...

_____
_____
_____
_____
_____
_____
_____
_____
_____
_____

One thing I wish I had handled differently was ...

_____
_____
_____
_____
_____
_____
_____
_____
_____
_____

I helped ...

_____
_____
_____
_____
_____
_____
_____
_____
_____

I got frustrated when ...

_____
_____
_____
_____
_____
_____
_____
_____
_____

Now, I also need to tell you about ...

_____
_____
_____
_____
_____
_____
_____
_____
_____

EXTRAS

It makes my parents mad when I ...

_____
_____
_____
_____
_____
_____
_____
_____
_____
_____

My parents would describe me as ...

_____
_____
_____
_____
_____
_____
_____
_____
_____
_____

A word that my friends would use to describe me is ...

_____
_____
_____
_____
_____
_____
_____
_____
_____
_____

WHAT I DID TODAY, _____ 20____.

Today I ...

_____
_____
_____
_____
_____
_____
_____
_____
_____
_____
_____

I am proud about ...

_____
_____
_____
_____
_____
_____
_____
_____
_____
_____

One thing I wish I had handled differently was ...

_____
_____
_____
_____
_____
_____
_____
_____
_____

I helped ...

_____
_____
_____
_____
_____
_____
_____
_____
_____

I got frustrated when ...

_____
_____
_____
_____
_____
_____
_____
_____
_____

Now, I also need to tell you about ...

_____
_____
_____
_____
_____
_____
_____
_____
_____
_____

EXTRAS

It makes my parents really happy when I ...

_____
_____
_____
_____
_____
_____
_____
_____
_____
_____

The best thing about Halloween is ...

_____
_____
_____
_____
_____
_____
_____
_____
_____
_____

If I could have any outfit it would be ...

_____
_____
_____
_____
_____
_____
_____
_____
_____
_____

WHAT I DID TODAY, _____ 20____.

Today I ...

_____
_____
_____
_____
_____
_____
_____
_____
_____
_____
_____

I am proud about ...

_____
_____
_____
_____
_____
_____
_____
_____
_____
_____

One thing I wish I had handled differently was ...

_____
_____
_____
_____
_____
_____
_____
_____
_____
_____

I helped ...

_____
_____
_____
_____
_____
_____
_____
_____
_____
_____

I got frustrated when ...

_____
_____
_____
_____
_____
_____
_____
_____
_____
_____

Now, I also need to tell you about ...

_____
_____
_____
_____
_____
_____
_____
_____
_____
_____

EXTRAS

I think my parents would be really proud of me if I tried ...

_____

_____

_____

_____

_____

_____

_____

_____

_____

I know I already make my parents proud when I ...

_____

_____

_____

_____

_____

_____

_____

_____

_____

It gives me a stomachache just to THINK about ...

_____

_____

_____

_____

_____

_____

_____

_____

_____

WHAT I DID TODAY, _____ 20____.

Today I ...

_____

_____

_____

_____

_____

_____

_____

_____

_____

I am proud about ...

_____

_____

_____

_____

_____

_____

_____

_____

_____

One thing I wish I had handled differently was ...

_____

_____

_____

_____

_____

_____

_____

_____

_____

I helped ...

_____

_____

_____

_____

_____

_____

_____

_____

_____

I got frustrated when ...

_____

_____

_____

_____

_____

_____

_____

_____

_____

Now, I also need to tell you about ...

_____

_____

_____

_____

_____

_____

_____

_____

_____

EXTRAS

One thing I tried that I never want to try again is ...

_____
_____
_____
_____
_____
_____
_____
_____
_____
_____

My favorite part of the day is ...

_____
_____
_____
_____
_____
_____
_____
_____
_____
_____

The most interesting part of school is ...

_____
_____
_____
_____
_____
_____
_____
_____
_____

WHAT I DID TODAY, _____ 20____.

Today I ...

_____
_____
_____
_____
_____
_____
_____
_____
_____
_____

I am proud about ...

_____
_____
_____
_____
_____
_____
_____
_____
_____

One thing I wish I had handled differently was ...

_____
_____
_____
_____
_____
_____
_____
_____
_____

I helped ...

_____
_____
_____
_____
_____
_____
_____
_____
_____

I got frustrated when ...

_____
_____
_____
_____
_____
_____
_____
_____
_____

Now, I also need to tell you about ...

_____
_____
_____
_____
_____
_____
_____
_____
_____
_____

EXTRAS

I can't believe my mom ...

_____

_____

_____

_____

_____

_____

_____

_____

_____

The best thing about my friends is ...

_____

_____

_____

_____

_____

_____

_____

_____

_____

I hope one day my dad will ...

_____

_____

_____

_____

_____

_____

_____

_____

_____

WHAT I DID TODAY, _____ 20____ .

Today I ...

_____
_____
_____
_____
_____
_____
_____
_____
_____
_____
_____
_____

I am proud about ...

_____
_____
_____
_____
_____
_____
_____
_____
_____
_____

One thing I wish I had handled differently was ...

_____
_____
_____
_____
_____
_____
_____
_____
_____

I helped ...

_____

_____

_____

_____

_____

_____

_____

_____

I got frustrated when ...

_____

_____

_____

_____

_____

_____

_____

_____

Now, I also need to tell you about ...

_____

_____

_____

_____

_____

_____

_____

_____

EXTRAS

I feel sorry for people who ...

One embarrassing thing that happened to me was ...

I got over being embarrassed by ...

WHAT I DID TODAY, _____ 20____.

Today I ...

_____
_____
_____
_____
_____
_____
_____
_____
_____
_____

I am proud about ...

_____
_____
_____
_____
_____
_____
_____
_____
_____
_____

One thing I wish I had handled differently was ...

_____
_____
_____
_____
_____
_____
_____
_____
_____

I helped ...

_____

_____

_____

_____

_____

_____

_____

_____

I got frustrated when ...

_____

_____

_____

_____

_____

_____

_____

_____

Now, I also need to tell you about ...

_____

_____

_____

_____

_____

_____

_____

_____

_____

EXTRAS

The most boring thing I ever remember doing was ...

_____
_____
_____
_____
_____
_____
_____
_____
_____
_____

The way I got through being so bored was ...

_____
_____
_____
_____
_____
_____
_____
_____
_____
_____

I don't understand why everyone likes ...

_____
_____
_____
_____
_____
_____
_____
_____
_____
_____

WHAT I DID TODAY, _____ 20____ .

Today I ...

_____
_____
_____
_____
_____
_____
_____
_____
_____
_____
_____

I am proud about ...

_____
_____
_____
_____
_____
_____
_____
_____
_____
_____

One thing I wish I had handled differently was ...

_____
_____
_____
_____
_____
_____
_____
_____
_____
_____

I helped ...

_____
_____
_____
_____
_____
_____
_____
_____
_____

I got frustrated when ...

_____
_____
_____
_____
_____
_____
_____
_____
_____

Now, I also need to tell you about ...

_____
_____
_____
_____
_____
_____
_____
_____
_____
_____

EXTRAS

I wish my parents ...

_____

_____

_____

_____

_____

_____

_____

_____

_____

_____

I wish my brother/sister ...

_____

_____

_____

_____

_____

_____

_____

_____

_____

I wish I ...

_____

_____

_____

_____

_____

_____

_____

_____

WHAT I DID TODAY, _____ 20 _____.

Today I ...

_____
_____
_____
_____
_____
_____
_____
_____
_____
_____

I am proud about ...

_____
_____
_____
_____
_____
_____
_____
_____
_____

One thing I wish I had handled differently was ...

_____
_____
_____
_____
_____
_____
_____
_____
_____

I helped ...

_____
_____
_____
_____
_____
_____
_____
_____
_____

I got frustrated when ...

_____
_____
_____
_____
_____
_____
_____
_____
_____
_____

Now, I also need to tell you about ...

_____
_____
_____
_____
_____
_____
_____
_____
_____
_____
_____

EXTRAS

My favorite game is ...

_____

_____

_____

_____

_____

_____

_____

_____

_____

_____

If I could ask my mom/dad one question, it would be ...

_____

_____

_____

_____

_____

_____

_____

_____

_____

_____

The reason I can't ask them is ...

_____

_____

_____

_____

_____

_____

_____

_____

_____

_____

WHAT I DID TODAY, _____ 20___.

Today I ...

_____
_____
_____
_____
_____
_____
_____
_____
_____
_____

I am proud about ...

_____
_____
_____
_____
_____
_____
_____
_____
_____
_____

One thing I wish I had handled differently was ...

_____
_____
_____
_____
_____
_____
_____
_____
_____

I helped ...

_____
_____
_____
_____
_____
_____
_____
_____
_____

I got frustrated when ...

_____
_____
_____
_____
_____
_____
_____
_____
_____

Now, I also need to tell you about ...

_____
_____
_____
_____
_____
_____
_____
_____
_____

EXTRAS

The one thing I wish I could tell my parents is ...

_____
_____
_____
_____
_____
_____
_____
_____
_____
_____

The reason I can't is ...

_____
_____
_____
_____
_____
_____
_____
_____
_____
_____

If I did tell them ...

_____
_____
_____
_____
_____
_____
_____
_____
_____

WHAT I DID TODAY, _____ 20____.

Today I ...

_____
_____
_____
_____
_____
_____
_____
_____
_____

I am proud about ...

_____
_____
_____
_____
_____
_____
_____
_____
_____

One thing I wish I had handled differently was ...

_____
_____
_____
_____
_____
_____
_____
_____
_____

I helped ...

_____
_____
_____
_____
_____
_____
_____
_____

I got frustrated when ...

_____
_____
_____
_____
_____
_____
_____
_____
_____

Now, I also need to tell you about ...

_____
_____
_____
_____
_____
_____
_____
_____
_____
_____

EXTRAS

The one thing I know my parents will always feel about me is ...

_____

_____

_____

_____

_____

_____

_____

_____

_____

The way I know that is ...

_____

_____

_____

_____

_____

_____

_____

_____

_____

Some of the kids at school are ...

_____

_____

_____

_____

_____

_____

_____

_____

_____

_____

WHAT I DID TODAY, _____ 20____ .

Today I ...

_____
_____
_____
_____
_____
_____
_____
_____
_____
_____

I am proud about ...

_____
_____
_____
_____
_____
_____
_____
_____
_____

One thing I wish I had handled differently was ...

_____
_____
_____
_____
_____
_____
_____
_____
_____

I helped ...

_____
_____
_____
_____
_____
_____
_____
_____
_____

I got frustrated when ...

_____
_____
_____
_____
_____
_____
_____
_____
_____

Now, I also need to tell you about ...

_____
_____
_____
_____
_____
_____
_____
_____
_____

EXTRAS

If I could be in the Olympics in any sport, I would choose ...

The stupidest thing I have ever said or done was ...

The funniest thing I ever did was ...

WHAT I DID TODAY, _____ 20_____ .

Today I ...

_____
_____
_____
_____
_____
_____
_____
_____
_____
_____

I am proud about ...

_____
_____
_____
_____
_____
_____
_____
_____
_____

One thing I wish I had handled differently was ...

_____
_____
_____
_____
_____
_____
_____
_____
_____

I helped ...

_____
_____
_____
_____
_____
_____
_____
_____
_____
_____

I got frustrated when ...

_____
_____
_____
_____
_____
_____
_____
_____
_____
_____
_____

Now, I also need to tell you about ...

_____
_____
_____
_____
_____
_____
_____
_____
_____
_____
_____
_____

EXTRAS

The worst thing about keeping secrets is ...

_____

_____

_____

_____

_____

_____

_____

_____

_____

_____

I think sleeping over at a friend's house is ...

_____

_____

_____

_____

_____

_____

_____

_____

_____

_____

I wish I weren't scared to ...

_____

_____

_____

_____

_____

_____

_____

_____

_____

_____

_____

WHAT I DID TODAY, _____ 20____ .

Today I ...

_____

_____

_____

_____

_____

_____

_____

_____

_____

I am proud about ...

_____

_____

_____

_____

_____

_____

_____

_____

_____

One thing I wish I had handled differently was ...

_____

_____

_____

_____

_____

_____

_____

_____

I helped ...

_____

_____

_____

_____

_____

_____

_____

_____

_____

I got frustrated when ...

_____

_____

_____

_____

_____

_____

_____

_____

_____

Now, I also need to tell you about ...

_____

_____

_____

_____

_____

_____

_____

_____

_____

_____

EXTRAS

My favorite thing to do outside is ...

_____

_____

_____

_____

_____

_____

_____

_____

_____

_____

When I am home alone I like to ...

_____

_____

_____

_____

_____

_____

_____

_____

_____

_____

One thing I should work harder on is ...

_____

_____

_____

_____

_____

_____

_____

_____

_____

_____

WHAT I DID TODAY, _____ 20____.

Today I ...

_____
_____
_____
_____
_____
_____
_____
_____
_____
_____
_____

I am proud about ...

_____
_____
_____
_____
_____
_____
_____
_____
_____
_____

One thing I wish I had handled differently was ...

_____
_____
_____
_____
_____
_____
_____
_____
_____
_____

I helped ...

_____
_____
_____
_____
_____
_____
_____
_____

I got frustrated when ...

_____
_____
_____
_____
_____
_____
_____
_____
_____

Now, I also need to tell you about ...

_____
_____
_____
_____
_____
_____
_____
_____
_____

EXTRAS

I hope I am the first one of my friends to ...

_____
_____
_____
_____
_____
_____
_____
_____
_____
_____

I hope I will be the last one of my friends to ...

_____
_____
_____
_____
_____
_____
_____
_____
_____
_____

One thing my teachers like about me is ...

_____
_____
_____
_____
_____
_____
_____
_____
_____
_____

WHAT I DID TODAY, _____ 20____ .

Today I ...

_____
_____
_____
_____
_____
_____
_____
_____
_____
_____

I am proud about ...

_____
_____
_____
_____
_____
_____
_____
_____
_____
_____

One thing I wish I had handled differently was ...

_____
_____
_____
_____
_____
_____
_____
_____
_____

I helped ...

_____
_____
_____
_____
_____
_____
_____
_____
_____

I got frustrated when ...

_____
_____
_____
_____
_____
_____
_____
_____
_____

Now, I also need to tell you about ...

_____
_____
_____
_____
_____
_____
_____
_____
_____
_____

EXTRAS

I would like to learn more about ...

_____
_____
_____
_____
_____
_____
_____
_____
_____
_____

One way I could help the environment is ...

_____
_____
_____
_____
_____
_____
_____
_____
_____
_____

I make my parents laugh when I ...

_____
_____
_____
_____
_____
_____
_____
_____
_____
_____

WHAT I DID TODAY, _____ 20____.

Today I ...

_____
_____
_____
_____
_____
_____
_____
_____
_____

I am proud about ...

_____
_____
_____
_____
_____
_____
_____
_____
_____

One thing I wish I had handled differently was ...

_____
_____
_____
_____
_____
_____
_____
_____
_____

I helped ...

_____
_____
_____
_____
_____
_____
_____
_____
_____
_____

I got frustrated when ...

_____
_____
_____
_____
_____
_____
_____
_____
_____
_____

Now, I also need to tell you about ...

_____
_____
_____
_____
_____
_____
_____
_____
_____
_____

EXTRAS

The meanest thing I ever did was ...

_____

_____

_____

_____

_____

_____

_____

_____

_____

The reason I did it was ...

_____

_____

_____

_____

_____

_____

_____

_____

_____

I wish that instead I had ...

_____

_____

_____

_____

_____

_____

_____

_____

_____

WHAT I DID TODAY, _____ 20____.

Today I ...

_____
_____
_____
_____
_____
_____
_____
_____
_____
_____
_____

I am proud about ...

_____
_____
_____
_____
_____
_____
_____
_____
_____
_____

One thing I wish I had handled differently was ...

_____
_____
_____
_____
_____
_____
_____
_____
_____
_____

I helped ...

_____
_____
_____
_____
_____
_____
_____
_____
_____

I got frustrated when ...

_____
_____
_____
_____
_____
_____
_____
_____
_____
_____

Now, I also need to tell you about ...

_____
_____
_____
_____
_____
_____
_____
_____
_____
_____
_____

EXTRAS

It must be hard to be a mom because ...

_____
_____
_____
_____
_____
_____
_____
_____
_____

The best part of being a mom is probably ...

_____
_____
_____
_____
_____
_____
_____
_____
_____

The best birthday party I ever went to was ...

_____
_____
_____
_____
_____
_____
_____
_____

WHAT I DID TODAY, _____ 20____.

Today I ...

_____
_____
_____
_____
_____
_____
_____
_____
_____
_____
_____

I am proud about ...

_____
_____
_____
_____
_____
_____
_____
_____
_____
_____

One thing I wish I had handled differently was ...

_____
_____
_____
_____
_____
_____
_____
_____
_____
_____

I helped ...

_____
_____
_____
_____
_____
_____
_____
_____
_____
_____

I got frustrated when ...

_____
_____
_____
_____
_____
_____
_____
_____
_____
_____
_____

Now, I also need to tell you about ...

_____
_____
_____
_____
_____
_____
_____
_____
_____
_____
_____

EXTRAS

My favorite hairstyle is ...

_____
_____
_____
_____
_____
_____
_____
_____
_____
_____

People say that when I was a baby I was ...

_____
_____
_____
_____
_____
_____
_____
_____
_____
_____

People say that when I am older I will be ...

_____
_____
_____
_____
_____
_____
_____
_____
_____
_____

WHAT I DID TODAY, _____ 20____.

Today I ...

_____

_____

_____

_____

_____

_____

_____

_____

_____

_____

I am proud about ...

_____

_____

_____

_____

_____

_____

_____

_____

_____

One thing I wish I had handled differently was ...

_____

_____

_____

_____

_____

_____

_____

_____

_____

I helped ...

_____

_____

_____

_____

_____

_____

_____

_____

I got frustrated when ...

_____

_____

_____

_____

_____

_____

_____

_____

Now, I also need to tell you about ...

_____

_____

_____

_____

_____

_____

_____

_____

_____

EXTRAS

I wish my dad would spend more time ...

_____
_____
_____
_____
_____
_____
_____
_____
_____
_____
_____

I wonder when I will ...

_____
_____
_____
_____
_____
_____
_____
_____
_____
_____
_____

If I could be any age for the rest of my life it would be ...

_____
_____
_____
_____
_____
_____
_____
_____
_____
_____
_____

WHAT I DID TODAY, _____ 20____.

Today I ...

_____
_____
_____
_____
_____
_____
_____
_____
_____
_____
_____

I am proud about ...

_____
_____
_____
_____
_____
_____
_____
_____
_____

One thing I wish I had handled differently was ...

_____
_____
_____
_____
_____
_____
_____
_____
_____

I helped ...

_____
_____
_____
_____
_____
_____
_____
_____
_____

I got frustrated when ...

_____
_____
_____
_____
_____
_____
_____
_____
_____

Now, I also need to tell you about ...

_____
_____
_____
_____
_____
_____
_____
_____
_____
_____

EXTRAS

I think my friends spend too much time worrying about ...

_____
_____
_____
_____
_____
_____
_____
_____
_____
_____

I think I spend too much time thinking about ...

_____
_____
_____
_____
_____
_____
_____
_____
_____
_____

It relaxes me to ...

_____
_____
_____
_____
_____
_____
_____
_____
_____
_____

WHAT I DID TODAY, _____ 20____ .

Today I ...

_____
_____
_____
_____
_____
_____
_____
_____
_____
_____
_____

I am proud about ...

_____
_____
_____
_____
_____
_____
_____
_____
_____
_____

One thing I wish I had handled differently was ...

_____
_____
_____
_____
_____
_____
_____
_____
_____
_____

I helped ...

_____
_____
_____
_____
_____
_____
_____
_____
_____

I got frustrated when ...

_____
_____
_____
_____
_____
_____
_____
_____
_____
_____

Now, I also need to tell you about ...

_____
_____
_____
_____
_____
_____
_____
_____
_____
_____

EXTRAS

I think I would fight with my parents less if they ...

_____

_____

_____

_____

_____

_____

_____

_____

_____

One thing I really like to do with my parents is ...

_____

_____

_____

_____

_____

_____

_____

_____

If I could only bring three things with me to a deserted island, they would be ...

_____

_____

_____

_____

_____

_____

_____

_____

WHAT I DID TODAY, _____ 20___ .

Today I ...

_____
_____
_____
_____
_____
_____
_____
_____
_____
_____
_____

I am proud about ...

_____
_____
_____
_____
_____
_____
_____
_____
_____
_____

One thing I wish I had handled differently was ...

_____
_____
_____
_____
_____
_____
_____
_____
_____
_____

I helped ...

_____
_____
_____
_____
_____
_____
_____
_____
_____

I got frustrated when ...

_____
_____
_____
_____
_____
_____
_____
_____
_____

Now, I also need to tell you about ...

_____
_____
_____
_____
_____
_____
_____
_____
_____

EXTRAS

I think I need more ...

_____
_____
_____
_____
_____
_____
_____
_____
_____
_____

I think I need less...

_____
_____
_____
_____
_____
_____
_____
_____
_____
_____

I think it is cool when people....

_____
_____
_____
_____
_____
_____
_____
_____
_____
_____
_____

WHAT I DID TODAY, _____ 20___.

Today I ...

_____
_____
_____
_____
_____
_____
_____
_____
_____
_____
_____

I am proud about ...

_____
_____
_____
_____
_____
_____
_____
_____
_____
_____

One thing I wish I had handled differently was ...

_____
_____
_____
_____
_____
_____
_____
_____
_____
_____

I helped ...

_____
_____
_____
_____
_____
_____
_____
_____
_____

I got frustrated when ...

_____
_____
_____
_____
_____
_____
_____
_____
_____

Now, I also need to tell you about ...

_____
_____
_____
_____
_____
_____
_____
_____
_____

EXTRAS

My favorite song is ...

_____

_____

_____

_____

_____

_____

_____

_____

_____

By the end of the school year I really hope I will have learned ...

_____

_____

_____

_____

_____

_____

_____

_____

_____

If I don't understand something in school I ...

_____

_____

_____

_____

_____

_____

_____

_____

_____

WHAT I DID TODAY, _____ 20____.

Today I ...

_____
_____
_____
_____
_____
_____
_____
_____
_____
_____

I am proud about ...

_____
_____
_____
_____
_____
_____
_____
_____
_____
_____

One thing I wish I had handled differently was ...

_____
_____
_____
_____
_____
_____
_____
_____
_____

I helped ...

_____
_____
_____
_____
_____
_____
_____
_____
_____

I got frustrated when ...

_____
_____
_____
_____
_____
_____
_____
_____
_____

Now, I also need to tell you about ...

_____
_____
_____
_____
_____
_____
_____
_____
_____

EXTRAS

I can't imagine having to ...

_____
_____
_____
_____
_____
_____
_____
_____
_____
_____

I am strong because I ...

_____
_____
_____
_____
_____
_____
_____
_____
_____
_____

If my pet could talk, it would say ...

_____
_____
_____
_____
_____
_____
_____
_____
_____
_____

WHAT I DID TODAY, _____ 20____ .

Today I ...

_____
_____
_____
_____
_____
_____
_____
_____
_____
_____

I am proud about ...

_____
_____
_____
_____
_____
_____
_____
_____
_____
_____

One thing I wish I had handled differently was ...

_____
_____
_____
_____
_____
_____
_____
_____
_____

I helped ...

_____
_____
_____
_____
_____
_____
_____
_____

I got frustrated when ...

_____
_____
_____
_____
_____
_____
_____
_____

Now, I also need to tell you about ...

_____
_____
_____
_____
_____
_____
_____
_____
_____

EXTRAS

My favorite thing to do on a Sunday morning is ...

_____
_____
_____
_____
_____
_____
_____
_____
_____
_____

The best gift I ever got was ...

_____
_____
_____
_____
_____
_____
_____
_____
_____
_____
_____

The best gift I ever gave was ...

_____
_____
_____
_____
_____
_____
_____
_____
_____
_____

WHAT I DID TODAY, _____ 20____ .

Today I ...

_____
_____
_____
_____
_____
_____
_____
_____
_____

I am proud about ...

_____
_____
_____
_____
_____
_____
_____
_____
_____

One thing I wish I had handled differently was ...

_____
_____
_____
_____
_____
_____
_____
_____
_____

I helped ...

_____
_____
_____
_____
_____
_____
_____
_____
_____

I got frustrated when ...

_____
_____
_____
_____
_____
_____
_____
_____
_____
_____

Now, I also need to tell you about ...

_____
_____
_____
_____
_____
_____
_____
_____
_____
_____

EXTRAS

When I am tired I like to...

_____
_____
_____
_____
_____
_____
_____
_____
_____
_____

What I liked about writing in this journal was ...

_____
_____
_____
_____
_____
_____
_____
_____
_____
_____

When I go back and read some things I have written, it makes me think ...

_____
_____
_____
_____
_____
_____
_____
_____
_____
_____

ABOUT THE AUTHOR

Susanna Blake Murphy and her two older sisters were raised by their father in Washington DC. She wishes she had adopted the practice of journaling as a child to help her through her tumultuous adolescent years. Murphy now lives outside of Boston with her husband, daughter, and son.